In the MARRY MONTH

THE BEST WEDDING AND MARRIAGE JOKES AND CARTOONS
from *The Joyful Noiseletter*
EDITED BY CAL AND ROSE SAMRA

BARBOUR
PUBLISHING

ISBN 978-1-61626-277-8

Published by Barbour Publishing, Inc., P.O. Box 719, Uhrichsville, Ohio 44683, www.barbourbooks.com

To purchase additional copies of this book, please see your local Christian bookstore or contact Barbour Publishing at the address or website noted above.

Our mission is to publish and distribute inspirational products offering exceptional value and biblical encouragement to the masses.

 Member of the
Evangelical Christian
Publishers Association

IF YOU'RE NOT ALLOWED TO LAUGH IN HEAVEN,
I DON'T WANT TO GO THERE.

MARTIN LUTHER

CONTENTS

CHRIST IS A GOD OF JOY. IT IS PLEASING TO
THE DEAR GOD WHENEVER THOU REJOICEST OR
LAUGHEST FROM THE BOTTOM OF THY HEART.

MARTIN LUTHER

Martin Luther was one of many Christians
from various faith traditions who greatly
valued humor. John Wesley, Charles H.
Spurgeon, G. K. Chesterton and many others
down through the centuries used humor as
a powerful bridge-building, evangelistic,
and healing tool.

For the past twenty-five years, *The Joyful
Noiseletter* has been providing subscribing
churches with jokes that pastors can tell and
rib-tickling humor and cartoons which are
reproducible in local church newsletters,
bulletins, and websites.

This book features some of *TJN's* best
wedding and marriage jokes and cartoons. The
copyrighted materials in this book are just for
laughs, and may not be reproduced in church
publications and websites.

But *subscribers* to *The Joyful Noiseletter*
have automatic permission to reproduce the
holy humor and cartoons in each issue of

the newsletter in their local church publications and websites. An annual subscription is $29, and may be ordered from *TJN's* website (www.joyfulnoiseletter.com) or by calling toll-free 1-800-877-2757.

Couples who pray and laugh together are more likely to stay together.

Enjoy!

CAL SAMRA, EDITOR
THE JOYFUL NOISELETTER

from JoyfulNoiseletter.com
© Ed Sullivan

INTRODUCTION

*While strolling through the park one day,
in the merry merry month of...*

Or wait...is that

*Something old,
Something new,
Something borrowed,
Something blue!*

Okay, so marriage is more than a romantic love song, and it's no laughing matter—but let's acknowledge that the wonderful institution benefits from a heaping order of smiles, giggles, snickers, snorts, and outright guffaws!

Wedded bliss is not for the faint of heart. Neither is it for the sole enjoyment of the young. Many an older pair have been known to thrive quite well in its all-encompassing embrace. As a matter of fact, the seniors among us could teach us a thing (or fifty) about how to make it to number fifty—with a giggle and a guffaw.

But what about the young? Undoubtedly, the newness of a flowing white gown and a tummy-tucking cummerbund are portents of things to come: aprons (at the stove or the grill), jacket pockets stuffed with "honey-do" reminders, and a blouse or shirt shoulder with the telltale signs of a baby's lunch.

The borrowing element of a very merry marriage is one of the distinguishing elements of a couple's understanding each other's DNA. It's not just, "Oh look, you have your dad's receding hairline" or "There you go. . .you sound just like your mother." Admit it, what you "borrowed" from the family gene pool is just as much a part of the "I do's" as the acceptance of a ring and a new last name.

Finally, there's the azure blue and wistful side of marriage. Along with the sky-blue moments, there is that indigo side of the equation when it takes a double dose of humor, patience, and God's grace.

It may be coincidence, but marriage began in a park-like setting. When the Creator sized up His accomplishment, he must have smiled broadly when He said, "It is good."

PAUL M. MILLER

1

"Did Adam and Eve have a prenuptial agreement?"

from JoyfulNoiseletter.com
© Tim Oliphant

IN THE BEGINNING—GOD:
Adam and Eve, Creation, a Rib, and This Holy Estate

There is nary a giraffe or chimpanzee alive today who can give an eyewitness account of that first knot-tying ceremony in the Garden of Eden.

Of course the Creator was present, and He gave us a you-are-there account in two chapters of the book of Genesis. No fashion editor attended to describe the bride's gown—but we do have all the whys and wherefores of God's mating-up humankind.

Since that time, plenty of imaginative conversations between God and the first groom have been written. Remember this one?

"I'm lonely," Adam told God in the garden. "I need to have someone around for company."

"Okay," replied God. "I'll give you the perfect companion. She is beautiful, intelligent, and gracious—she'll cook and clean for you and never say a cross word."

"Sounds great," Adam said. "But what's she going to cost me?"

"An arm and a leg," answered God.

"That's pretty steep," replied Adam. "What can I get for a rib?"

It turned out pretty well in the end.

BUT WILL IT LAST?

Rev. Mark A. Katrick, pastor of Immanuel United Church of Christ, Zanesville, Ohio, passes on this verbal blooper at a wedding:

The bride and groom had chosen Mark 10:6–9, and Pastor Katrick dutifully began to read: "But in the beginning, at the time of creation, God made them male and female. As the scripture says, a man will leave his wife and be united with his mother. . . ."

ONE-LINERS

What a good thing Adam had—when he said a good thing, he knew nobody had said it before.

MARK TWAIN

Adam to Eve: "I'll wear the plants in this family!"

A RiB-TiCKLER

A little boy came home from Sunday school very excited about the lesson he had read about the creation and how Eve was taken from Adam's side. A few days later, he came home from school in a seemingly distressed mood. When his mother asked what was wrong, he replied: "My side hurts. I think I'm going to have a wife."

NORA TREECE
TRUSSVILLE, ALABAMA

THE OPTIONS?

Eve: Do you still love me, Adam?
Adam: Who else?

WOE IS ME

Adam surely had his troubles,
but it never could be said
he had to bear Eve telling him
of the man she might have wed.

PASTOR DONALD PROUT
WEST PRESTON, VICTORIA, AUSTRALIA

ADAM'S VALENTINE TO EVE

Adam's Valentine to Eve
did not imply a choice.
The modern girls can pick and choose
from many charming boys.
His verse ran thus:
"Dear Miss, I'm Adam.
I'm all there is to make you, Madam."

LOIS GRANT PALCHES
CONCORD, MASSACHUSETTS

TEN REASONS WHY ADAM WAS THE MOST FORTUNATE OF MEN

1. He was the only man who has never been compared to the man she could have married.
2. He had no in-laws to drop in unexpectedly.
3. There were no Joneses for him to keep up with.
4. There were no credit cards or shopping centers.
5. He never had his dinner interrupted by telephone sales calls.
6. He got away with wearing a simple wardrobe.
7. He never had to shovel snow.
8. If he had gone bald, who would have known that wasn't normal?
9. There was no "standard" weight and height table.
10. When God asked, "Adam, where are you?" he replied, "The woman you gave me is reading the map."

UNKNOWN

from JoyfulNoiseletter.com
© Ed Sullivan

A Missing Leaf

A Presbyterian minister always carefully prepared his sermons word for word and placed
them in a loose-leaf binder to deliver Sunday
morning. One Saturday night, his son, just
for fun, removed a sheet from the scripted
sermon.

The following morning, the preacher
was carefully reading his sermon to the
congregation: "...and Adam said to Eve..."
He turned the page and discovered it was
missing.

Perplexed, the minister looked at the
congregation and said, "There must be a leaf
missing here."

Humorist Carroll Lamb
via George Goldtrap
Ormond-by-the-Sea, Florida

BiBLiMERiCKS

Lois Blanchard Eades of Dickenson, Tennessee, writes "Biblimericks." Here is one she passed on to *The Joyful Noiseletter*:

When Eve gave the apple to Adam,
They did what Jehovah forbade 'em.
As might be expected,
When they were detected,
He said, "Don't blame me, blame the Madam."

from JoyfulNoiseletter.com
© Ed Sullivan

I'm All Yours in Buttons and Bows:
Birds and Bees, Dating, and He vs. She

When the subjects of love, dating, and gender come up, a sense of humor is of utmost importance. The first date is a particularly tender subject, as are most issues concerning our courting rituals.

A nameless young lady once poured out her heart to her mother: "It was my first date with [name withheld to protect the accused], and I had shown the patience of a saint as he babbled on and on about his hobbies, his pet peeves, his other girlfriends, his driving techniques, and even the standard he uses to select a barber. Finally, he came up for air and said, 'But enough about me. Let's talk about you.' Well, I breathed a sigh of relief—then before I could open my mouth, he continued, 'What do *you* think about me?'"

There really *are* differences between male and female. And aren't we glad there are?

GENDER DIFFERENCES

A man will pay two dollars for a one dollar item he wants. A woman will pay one dollar for a two dollar item she doesn't want.

A woman worries about the future until she gets a husband. A man never worries about the future until he gets a wife.

A successful man is one who can make more money than his wife can spend. A successful woman is one who can find such a man.

A woman marries a man expecting him to change, but he doesn't. A man marries a woman expecting that she won't change, and she does.

Men wake up as good looking as they were when they went to bed. Women somehow deteriorate during the night.

Any married man should forget his mistakes—there's no use in two people remembering the same thing.

Guess what? There are exceptions to every rule.

UNKNOWN

WHEN IT ALL STARTED

Rev. George Martin of Rosemount, Minnesota, tells this story:

"One Sunday morning, just before the recessional, I realized I didn't have my church bulletin. I needed to see the page for the closing prayer and the closing hymn number.

"I leaned over and quietly asked one of the boy acolytes for his bulletin. At first he seemed reluctant to hand me his bulletin, but then he did.

"I found the right page for the closing prayer and then the closing hymn number. As we started the recessional, I flipped the bulletin over and saw a little note.

"One of the two boy acolytes had written to the other about the third acolyte, a girl named Kristie. The note said, 'What kind of perfume does Kristie have? She sure smells good.'"

LOOK OUT, HERE SHE COMES!

After bishop emeritus Kenneth Povish of
Lansing, Michigan, instituted at his parish
a weekly litany of divine praises of God for
the holiness of the saints, a young mother
attended with her son, a third grader.

After church the boy asked his mother,
"What is a spouse?"

"A spouse is somebody's husband or
wife," the mother replied. "Why do you ask?"

"What does 'most chaste spouse' mean?"
the boy asked.

"That means St. Joseph was a good, pure,
and holy husband," the mother answered.
"What do you think 'most chaste spouse'
means?"

Rather reluctantly the boy finally replied,
"Well, I think it means that all the women
were after him, but Mary got him in the end."

HARRIET ADAMS
MORTON, PENNSYLVANIA

THE HE VS. SHE ELEMENT

The Wise Men were truly wise men. Unlike most men, they stopped to ask for directions.

GEORGE E. FRANKE
WAUKEGAN, ILLINOIS

LOVE KNOW-HOW

On the first date, most people just tell each other lies, and that usually gets them interested enough to go for a second date.

TOM, AGE 9

A lady inserted an ad in the classifieds: "Husband Wanted!"

The next day she received two hundred letters.

They all said the same thing: "You can have mine."

DONNA LAMBERT
ALBUQUERQUE, NEW MEXICO

Why do brides buy their wedding gowns, and grooms rent their wedding suits?

Where love radiates its joy, there we have a feast.

JOHN CHRYSOSTOM (407 AD)

Beware: A study shows that 35 percent of the people who use personal ads for dating are already married.

You know you're in love when you're willing to share your ATM PIN number.

A guy knows he's in love when he loses interest in his car for a couple of days.

Love may be blind, but marriage is a real eye-opener.

UNKNOWN

A Single Woman's Prayer

Now I lay me down to sleep,
Please don't send me any more creeps.
Please just send me one good man—
One without a wedding band.

UNKNOWN

Males, Ugh!

After Sunday school, a little girl was telling her parents that the boys in her class were acting silly. "I hate boys!" she exclaimed.

Then, after some reflection, she added, "But I still love Jesus, even though He's a boy."

JEFF TOTTEN
LAKE CHARLES, LOUISIANA

Sour Grapes

After the May funeral of one of his parishioners, ninety-four-year-old Hazel von Jeschki, Fr. John Fetterman, rector at Grace Episcopal Church in Madison, Wisconsin, noted in the church bulletin that she had left very specific written instructions for her funeral service. The woman, who had never married, wrote: "There will be no male pallbearers. They wouldn't take me out when I was alive; I don't want them to take me out when I'm dead."

Dogs vs. Your Husband-to-Be

Both take up too much space on the bed.
Both have irrational fears about vacuum cleaning.
Both are threatened by their own kind.
Both mark their territory.
Neither does any dishes.
Neither of them notices when you get your hair cut.
Both are suspicious of the postman.
Neither understands what you see in cats.

"We'd like to tie the knot after years of
stringing each other along."

from JoyfulNoiseletter.com
© Jonny Hawkins

GENDER DESCRIPTIONS

Two adjacent signs seen at the top of a large bookshelf in a Christian bookstore in Decatur, Illinois:

WOMEN
HEALTH/AGING

MEN
DEATH/SUFFERING

DATING ADVICE

You don't have to worry about avoiding temptation as you grow older, because it will avoid you.

PATTY WOOTEN
SANTA CRUZ, CALIFORNIA

What the New Wife Learned About her Groom

♥ Phone conversations are over in thirty seconds flat.
♥ A five-day vacation requires only one suitcase.
♥ Dry cleaners and haircutters don't rob you blind.
♥ Wedding plans take care of themselves.
♥ If someone forgets to invite you to do something, he or she can still be your friend.
♥ Your underwear cost ten dollars for a three-pack.
♥ Everything on your face stays its original color.
♥ Three pairs of shoes are more than enough.
♥ You can quietly watch a game with your buddy for hours without ever thinking: "He must be mad at me."
♥ Wedding dress—$2,000. Tuxedo rental—$75.
♥ If another guy shows up at the party in the same outfit, you just might become lifelong friends.

- ♥ Your pals can be trusted never to trap you with "So. . .notice anything different?"
- ♥ You are able to see wrinkles in your clothes.
- ♥ The same hairstyle lasts for years—maybe decades.
- ♥ One wallet and one pair of shoes, one color, all seasons.
- ♥ Christmas shopping can be accomplished for twenty-five relatives, on December 24—in forty-five minutes.

"Light up My Life"

"A happy man or woman is a radiant focus of good will, and their entrance into a room is as though another candle had been lighted."

ROBERT LOUIS STEVENSON
VIA S. E. EDWARDS
INDIANAPOLIS, INDIANA

UNLIKE THE GROOM-TO-BE

- ♥ You don't have to get up at 4 a.m. to enjoy your hobbies.
- ♥ You can get together with a friend to just talk.
- ♥ You can be creative with your hair, your clothes, your makeup. . .and where you put your furniture!
- ♥ Your day is not ruined when Team X fails to deliver.
- ♥ You are aware of other food groups besides steak and potatoes.
- ♥ You can answer most questions with, "I just know."
- ♥ Shopping can be your main form of exercise.
- ♥ You don't have to circle the block several times before asking for directions.
- ♥ You get flowers, chocolates, and jewelry as gifts.
- ♥ Someone someday may say to you, "You're beautiful."

KATHLEEN GARDISER
MOUNTAIN VIEW, CALIFORNIA

♥ Taxis stop for women.
♥ Women can cry and get off speeding tickets.
♥ Women have the ability to dress themselves.
♥ In any sport, women can congratulate a teammate without patting her behind.
♥ Women know when to stop and ask directions.
♥ If a woman forgets to shave, no one has to know.
♥ Women will never regret piercing their ears.
♥ Women got off the *Titanic* first.

ROBERTA LYON
MAITLAND, FLORIDA

♥ You can wear pink and yellow together, and everyone thinks it's cool.
♥ No one asks you to come over and help lay a new concrete sidewalk.

SUSAN TAYLOR
SALT LAKE CITY, UTAH

THE FAMILY CIRCUS

"Is it against the law to be the Valentine of
two different girls?"

from JoyfulNoiseletter.com

LOVE BUDS

Moonlight and roses are bound to fade
for every lover and every maid,
but the bond that holds in any weather
is learning how to laugh together.

AUTHOR UNKNOWN
VIA NORMA SIMS
EUSTIS, FLORIDA

MEDICARE ROMANCE

An eighty-seven-year-old man and his eighty-two-year-old girlfriend, both in an assisted-living home, decided to get married. They went for a walk to discuss the wedding, and passed a pharmacy.

They entered, and the man told the pharmacist, "We're going to get married. Do you sell blood pressure medication?"

"Yes, indeed," the pharmacist replied.

The woman asked, "Do you also sell walkers, vitamins, Geritol, and medicine for arthritis, rheumatism, sinus infections, and gout?"

"Sure do," the pharmacist replied.

"Fine," the man said. "We'd like to register here for our wedding gifts, please."

HEARD THESE ANONYMOUS MARRIAGE VIEWS BEFORE?

I love being married. I was single for a long time, and I just got tired of finishing my own sentences.

I'm excited about being married. I've never had a dental plan before.

After seven years of marriage, I'm sure of two things: First, never wallpaper together; and second, you'll need two bathrooms, both for her.

My parents have a very good marriage; they've been together forever. They've passed their gold and silver anniversaries. The next one is rust.

"Happy Valentine's Day! This is Sherry's answering service. At the sound of the beep, please leave your name, age, length of hair, and whether or not you have an earring."

SUBJECTS FOR a DATE

Billy is about to have his first date and is nervous about what to talk about. He asks his father for advice.

The father replies: "Son, there are three subjects that always work. Those topics are food, family, and philosophy."

Billy picks up his date and they go to an ice-cream shop. Root beer floats are ordered and sipped, but no one says a word.

Remembering his father's advice, Billy chooses his first topic.

He asks the girl, "Do you like spinach?" She answers, "no," and the silence continues.

After a few more uncomfortable minutes, Billy thinks back to his father's suggestions and selects the second item on the list. "Do you have a brother?" he asks. Again, the answer is "no." Silence reigns once again.

Finally, in desperation, Billy plays his last card. He again thinks of his father's advice and asks, "If you had a brother, would *he* like spinach?"

UNKNOWN

EARLY CONSIDERATION

Q: What is the penalty for bigamy?
A: You get two mothers-in-law.

CLIFF THOMAS
BELLE FOURCHE, SOUTH DAKOTA

CUPID'S ARROWS

I don't understand why Cupid was chosen
to represent Valentine's Day. When I think
about romance, the last thing on my mind is
a short, chubby toddler coming at me with a
weapon.

UNKNOWN

Love is what makes you smile when you're tired.

EMILY, AGE 5

3

"Marriage? Wait a minute while I run an instant background check…"

I WANT TO HOLD YOUR HAND:
Getting Serious, Question Popping, and "What Am I Getting Into?"

"Pop the question" is a quaint way of saying, "You know, I feel like a bowl of Orville

Redenbacher when I'm near you—my ears listen to your warm voice, which makes my heart melt like butter, causing me to shake from head to toe until my mind explodes with a desire to be as close to you as salt is to a bowl of popcorn."

Testimonials about preproposal nerves are legendary. Bible readers are aware of Old Testament characters who proposed marriage to charming young ladies, only to rue the day that they ever opened their mouths. The number one example, perhaps, was a guy named Jacob, who had eyes for Laban's daughter Rachel—well, read the whole sorry story for yourself in Genesis 29–31. Just remember, the only things popping in that tale were the veins in Jacob's neck after Laban tried to switch daughters on him.

By the way, it's been said that when you tell a girl, "I want to hold your hand," you are taking the first step toward dishpan digits.

ANOTHER DAD'S QUESTION

Father: And when he proposed, did you ask
      him to see me?
Daughter: He said he had seen you, but he
      still loved me.

SIGNS OF THE TIMES

People are getting more monogamous. But
there's a reluctance to get married, maybe
because it seems like you're not getting
married to her, you're getting married to her
lawyer.

Outdoor sign on Valentine's Day at Bound
Brook, New Jersey, United Methodist
Church:

> GOD IS A HOPELESS ROMANTIC.

REV. LEE VAN RENSBURG
MAPLEWOOD, NEW JERSEY

God created safe sex. He called it marriage.

REV. KARL KRAFT
MANTUA, NEW JERSEY

Keep your eyes wide open before marriage,
half shut afterwards.

BENJAMIN FRANKLIN

Too many couples marry for better or for
worse, but not for good.

GEORGE GOLDTRAP

A PRAYER FOR THE MARRIED

"Lord, when we are wrong, make us willing to
change. When we are right, make us easy to
live with."

PETER MARSHALL

"Too bad we didn't meet sooner."

BRIDE-TO-BE: KNOW
Thy GROOM-TO-BE

Once there was a little lad,
always in a rush.
In fact, in such a hurry
that he'd forget to flush.

His mother would remind him,
and sometimes she would scold.
And even when she threatened,
he'd forget what he'd been told.

One day exasperated,
she called up to the school,
told his teacher to send him home
so he could flush his stool.

On the playground was the culprit,
so Miss Marks yelled loud and clear
from a second story window,
these words for all to hear.

Never was a face more reddened.
never ran two feet so fast.
Surely, this third grader
had, a lesson, learned at last.

But many decades later,
his lawful wedded wife
has been known to say that he still leads
a fast and flushless life.

DONNA MADDUX COOPER
STILLWATER, OKLAHOMA

THE YOUNG AND THE DARKNESS

A five-year-old boy announced to his mother one day that he wanted to marry Sally, the little girl who lived next door.

"Well," his Mom replied, smiling, "you're both a little bit young for that, aren't you?"

"I've got it figured out, Mom," the boy said. "We can spend one week in my room and the next week in hers. It's right next door, so I can run home if I get scared of the dark."

"We met during the church icebreaker tonight. Will you marry us?"

LOVE REFLECTIONS

A group of kids in Sunday school were asked, "What is the meaning of love?" Answers:

♥ "There are two kinds of love—our love and God's love. But God makes both kinds of them."

♥ "When someone loves you, the way they say your name is different. You know that your name is safe in their mouth."

♥ "Love cards like Valentine's Day cards say stuff on them that we'd like to say ourselves, but we wouldn't be caught dead saying."

♥ "Love is when someone hurts you, and you get so mad but you don't yell at them because you know it would hurt their feelings."

♥ "When my grandmother got arthritis, she couldn't bend over and paint her toenails anymore. So my grandfather does it for her all the time, even when his hands got arthritis, too. That's love."

♥ "Love is when you tell a guy you like his shirt—then he wears it every day."

Strange—the groom is married in rented shoes. Here he is making a commitment for a lifetime, in shoes that have to be back by five thirty.

UNKNOWN

"Sheer joy is God's and this demands companionship."

THOMAS AQUINAS

CommoN WEDDiNG QUESTIoNS aND ANSWERS

Q: Is it all right to bring a date to the wedding?
A: Not if you are the groom.

Q: How many showers is the bride supposed to have?
A: At least one within a week of the wedding.

HIT OR MISS

The pastor proposed to a maiden.
She refused; gone was his bliss.
A widow in his church said,
"Ye received not 'cause you ask a miss."

PASTOR DONALD PROUT
WEST PRESTON, AUSTRALIA

THE RIGHT ONE

Attending a wedding, Lilli Vorse of Council Bluffs, Iowa, got these answers from two nine-year-old children who were responding to the question, "How do you decide whom to marry?"

A young girl replied, "No person really decides before they grow up who they're going to marry. God decided it all way before, and you get to find out who you're stuck with."

A young boy replied, "You've got to find somebody who likes the same stuff. So, if you like sports, she should like it that you like sports, and she should keep the chips and dip coming."

A CHANGE OF MIND

My dearest Susan:

Sweetie of my heart, I've been so desolate ever since I broke off our engagement. You can never know how devastated I've become.

Won't you please consider taking me back? You hold a very loving place in my heart, and no other woman can fill it. I can never find or marry another woman quite like you. Won't you please forgive me and let us make a new start. I love you so.

Yours always and truly,
John

P.S. Congratulations on winning the state lottery.

UNKNOWN (OR NOT ADMITTING)

WERE YOU THERE?

At age six, my granddaughter, Sophia, asked her mother if she had been at her mother and father's wedding. Mary, my daughter, smiled and said, 'No, Sophia. You weren't born yet."

Sophia was quiet for a moment and then firmly corrected her mother. "Yes I was," she said. "I just hadn't shown up yet."

ANTOINETTE BOSCO
BROOKFIELD, CONNECTICUT

A WEDDING (R.I.N.G.) GUIDE

So you want to get married! That is wonderful, but have you thoroughly planned your wedding? Use this Wedding Readiness Inventory Niftiness Guide (Wedding R.I.N.G. or just W.R.I.N.G., as in hands or neck) to determine how well you have made decisions that reflect the use of the latest of what's *in* for the important day.

Circle the letter that most applies. Give yourself one point for every "a," three for every "b," and five for every "c."

1. *Location*: (a) home church, (b) backyard rose garden, (c) coach section of DC-9

2. *Time of day*: (a) 1:30 p.m., (b) 6:30 p.m., (c) halftime of pro basketball game

3. *Officiant*: (a) minister, priest or rabbi, (b) mayor or judge, (c) grand pooh-bah of local Sons of Knights of Armadillos of Ponce de Leon

4. *Professional music*: (a) Wagner's "Wedding March," (b) Purcell's "Trumpet Voluntary, (c) Billy Joel's "We Didn't Start the Fire"

5. *Maid of honor*: (a) sister of bride, (b) friend of bride, (c) investment advisor of bride

6. *Best man*: (a) brother of bridegroom, (b) friend of bridegroom, (c) tax consultant of bridegroom

7. *Reception*: (a) church basement, (b) local Antelope Lodge, (c) Richfield Coliseum

8. *Vow*: (a) "Till death do us part," (b) "For richer or poorer," (c) "Okay, but you don't expect me to put you through grad school"

9. *Accompaniment*: (a) pipe organ, (b) guitar, c) boom box

10. *Reception band*: (a) polka group, (b) chamber ensemble, (c) boom box

11. *Father of the bride*: (a) walks bride down the aisle, (b) beams as bride walks with groom down aisle, (c) off moonlighting to pay for wedding

12. *Toasting of bride and groom*: (a) best man, (b) uncle of bride, (c) Jay Leno

13. *Honeymoon*: (a) Niagara Falls, (b) Poconos, (c) world cruise on private schooner

14. *Bridal gown*: (a) wearing mother's wedding dress, (b) in style of *Bride* magazine, (c) á la Tina Turner

15. *Tuxedo*: (a) black with white shirt, (b) white with pastel shirt, (c) pastel with no shirt

16. *Transportation from wedding*: (a) decorated family car, (b) stretch limousine, (c) Lear jet

17. *Photographer*: (a) Aunt Thelma's instant camera, (b) local professional, (c) *National Geographic* photo team

18. *In general*: (a) following family traditions, (b) mixing tradition with couple's own ideas, (c) aiming for spot on *Funniest Home Videos*.

If you scored 60–90 points, you have a good grasp of what is important to newlyweds of the 2000s and little grasp of anything else.

If you scored 18–59 points, don't expect ever to make the cover of *People* magazine, but it is much more likely that twenty years from now you won't need to have your subscriptions sent to separate addresses.

HUMORIST PAUL LINTERN IS A LUTHERAN PASTOR IN MANSFIELD, OHIO, AND A CONSULTING EDITOR TO *THE JOYFUL NOISELETTER*

Now Hear This

There is no government program nearly as effective as marriage in helping a family escape or avoid poverty.

COLUMNIST JOSEPH PERKINS
SAN DIEGO UNION-TRIBUNE

"And so the prince and princess got divorced, and their attorneys lived happily ever after."

LOVE IS. . .

Love is what makes you smile when you're tired. (Five-year-old girl)

Love is when your puppy licks your face even after you left him alone all day. (Four-year-old boy)

Love is when a girl puts on a perfume and a boy puts on shaving cologne and they go out and smell each other. (Five-year-old boy)

JODY DAVIS
INDIANAPOLIS, INDIANA

A PSaLm FoR ONE FITTiNG iNTo a WEDDiNG GOWN oR TUX

The Lord is my shepherd, I shall not want.
He maketh me lie down and do push-ups,
He giveth me sodium-free bread,
He restoreth my waistline,
He leadeth me past the refrigerator for mine own sake.

He maketh me partake of broccoli instead of
potatoes,
He leadeth me past the pizzeria.
Yea, though I walk through the bakery
I shall not falter, for Thou are with me;
with diet colas I am comforted.
Thou preparest a diet for me in the presence
of my enemies,
Thou anointest my lettuce with low-cal olive oil.
My cup will not overflow.
Surely Ry-Krisp and D-Zerta shall follow me
all the days of my life, and I shall live with the
pangs of hunger forever.

To Each His Own

The father of a young woman who was being
courted asked the suitor, "Young man, can you
support a family?"

"Well, no," the prospective groom
replied. "I was just planning to support your
daughter. The rest of you will have to fend for
yourselves."

LOWELL YODER
HOLLAND, OHIO

IS THIS COVERED IN THE VOWS?

Humorist Liz Curtis Higgs, of Louisiana, Kentucky, is a happily married mother of two youngsters, a popular speaker, and author of the hilarious book, *Only Angels Can Wing It*. She shared some of her thoughts with *The Joyful Noiseletter*:

The experts claim that romance drops 80 percent in the first two years of marriage. I don't think it took that long for most of us.

A couple of food fights ("What's for dinner? Not again!") one pair of socks too many on the floor, and it's curtains for candlelight and champagne.

My husband, Bill, and I followed tradition and kept the top of the wedding cake to enjoy on our first anniversary. We both took one bite and threw it away. Yuck! Major freezer burn.

The image of the "Perfect Little Woman" went out with home-delivery dry cleaning. Today's woman is often trying to hold down several duties at once: wife, mother, friend, daughter, employee, volunteer, caregiver for an aging parent, alto in the church choir, and T-ball coach.

As one woman said, "Now that I have it all, I'd like to give some of it back!"

PROBABLY NOT APROPOS

According to Reuters, the Prince of Wales can publicly confess to adultery and divorce his wife, but the only thing that would stand in the way of his becoming King of England and head of the Church of England would be his subsequent marriage to a Catholic.

This was clearly the work of a committee.

HOW TRUE

What would men be without women? Scarce, sir, mighty scarce.

MARK TWAIN

ThE HoNEymooN NaP

Rev. Estill Franklin, 103, a retired Methodist minister, and Fern Brown, 90, were married not long ago in the chapel at the Wesley Manor Retirement Village in Crawfordsville, Indiana. After the ceremony, the newlyweds took a honeymoon ride around town in a limousine, and returned to the retirement home for a small reception. When asked their plans for the rest of the day, the bride replied, "A nap. All of this has worn me out."

RICHARD HASSING
THE INDIANAPOLIS STAR

BiBLE BLooPER

An 1810 Bible translated a passage from Luke that reads, "If any hate not his own life" as "If any hate not their own wife."

ANN BALL
HOUSTON, TEXAS

SENIOR MOMENTS

At a church seniors' dinner, a widow and widower who had known each other for several years sat across from one another and carried on a cordial conversation.

Later, the widower mustered the courage to ask her, "Will you marry me?" Without hesitating, the widow said, "Yes." They then kissed and returned to their nearby homes.

The next morning, the perplexed widower awoke wondering if the widow had said "Yes" or "No."

He telephoned her and apologized for his failure of memory. "When I asked if you would marry me, did you say 'Yes' or 'No'?" he inquired.

The widow replied, "I said, 'Yes,' and I meant it with all my heart. I'm so glad you called. I couldn't remember who asked me."

VIA KATHY MCMANUS
HENDERSONVILLE, TENNESSEE

KiDS ON ROMANCE

These pearls from elementary school students came by way of *Joyful Noiseletter* consulting editor Gina Bridgeman of Scottsdale, Arizona:

When asked, "How can a stranger tell if two people are married?" an eight-year-old boy replied, "You might have to guess, based on whether they seem to be yelling at the same kids."

When asked, "How would you make a marriage work?" a ten-year-old boy replied, "Tell your wife that she looks pretty even if she looks like a truck."

AN ELDER'S PROPOSAL

A pastor was called to a local nursing home to perform a wedding. An anxious old man met him at the door. The pastor sat down to counsel the old man and asked several questions. "Do you love her?"

The old man replied, "Nope."

Is she a good Christian woman?"

"I don't know for sure," the old man answered.

"Does she have lots of money?" asked the pastor.

"I doubt it."

"Then why are you marrying her?" the preacher asked.

"'Cause she can drive at night," the old man said.

GEORGE GOLDTRAP

SPEAKING ABOUT SOLOMON

If you think you've got problems, just remember King Solomon had over one thousand wives and concubines. Do you have any idea how many birthdays and anniversaries he had to keep straight?

HARP TUNES

"The marriage of couples who harp at each other were not necessarily made in heaven."

CATHERINE HALL
PITTSBURGH, PENNSYLVANIA

"Best sermon on love I ever heard, Pastor."

from JoyfulNoiseletter.com
© Jonny Hawkins

AN UNNERVED WILLIAM JENNINGS BRYAN

When the famous politician and orator William Jennings Bryan (1860–1925) was a young man, he went to the home of the father of his prospective wife to ask him for her hand in marriage. Bryan was determined to impress the father by quoting from the Bible, and he chose this Proverb: "Whosoever findeth a wife findeth a good thing, and obtaineth favor of the Lord."

Bryan was unnerved when the father replied by quoting Paul, "He that marrieth doeth well, but he that marrieth not doeth better."

But Bryan, never at a loss for words, said, "Paul had no wife and Solomon had 700. Therefore, I believe Solomon ought to be the better judge as to marriage."

Rev. Dennis R. Fakes
Lindsborg, Kansas

4

Bronco Marries
The Coach's Daughter

from JoyfulNoiseletter.com
© Steve Phelps

The old Folks at Home:
Parents, Relatives, In-Laws,
and an Outlaw or Two

Stephen Foster, composer of the familiar song
that begins, "Way down upon the Swanee
River," knew exactly why he moved "far, far
away"—his wife-to-be didn't want to be a
daughter-in-law, or inherit all those "old folks
at home."

It may have been Aristotle (or some kin of his), when confronted with the relative entanglements of marriage, who declared, "It's all Greek to me." Of course, those ancient philosophers were all confirmed bachelors. You could tell by the food stains on their togas.

Joking aside, what would love and marriage be without familial support? It would cost the bride a whole lot of cash, and the groom would be weeping over his checkbook long after his tux was returned to the rental shop.

Though the Good Book tells a young man to leave mom and dad's home and begin his own family (Matthew 19:4–6), it also advises him to "repay. . .parents and grandparents, for this is pleasing to God" (1 Timothy 5:4).

High Blood Pressure

When Doc Smith remarked on a newlywed patient's extraordinarily ruddy complexion, the patient said, "High blood pressure, Doc. It comes from my family."

"Your mother's side or your father's?"

"Neither," the patient replied, "it's from my wife's family."

"Oh come now, how could you get high blood pressure from your wife's family?"

The new husband sighed, "You oughta meet 'em sometimes, Doc!"

I'm the Father of the Bride

Fr. John Trimbur, pastor of St. John the Baptist Catholic Church, Campbell, Ohio, passed on the following card that the father of the bride gave him at a wedding: "Nobody's paying much attention to me today. But I can assure you that I am getting my fair share of attention, for the banks and several business firms are watching me very closely."

PASSING THE PLATE

At a church wedding, an usher began passing the collection plate and encountered some perplexed faces. "I know it's unusual," he explained, "but the father of the bride requested it."

DONNA LAMBERT

ON THE SOCIETY PAGE

"The bride was given in marriage by her father, wearing her mother's wedding gown."

VIA REV. KARL R. KRAFT

From the *Wellington Weekly News* in England: "The bridegroom's mother wore a two-piece purple and jade suit with purple accessories. The bride's mother wore a hat."

THE ANGLICAN DIGEST

LINCOLN'S FIANCÉE

Shortly before he was married, someone asked Abraham Lincoln about his fiancée's family name.

"The Todds are very important people," Lincoln replied. "They require two *d*s at the end of their name. The Almighty is content with one."

NOTHING BUT THE TRUTH

"Laugh and your husband laughs with you; weep and get what you want."

CHARLES J. MILAZZO
ST. PETERSBURG, FLORIDA

A little boy asked his father, "Daddy, how much does it cost to get married?"

Dad replied, "I don't know, son. I'm still paying."

The father was a grouch. When a young man told him he would like to marry his daughter, the father replied, irritably, "You're telling me that you want to become my son-in-law?"

"Not really," the young man said, "but if I marry your daughter, I don't see how I can avoid it."

OHIO MOTORIST

ALL ABOUT KIDS

Our four-year-old granddaughter was telling me about her aunt's wedding, which she attended. "Grandma," she said, "the minister asked my aunt if she would take this awful man to be her husband."

JEAN STRAWSINE
PRESCOTT, MICHIGAN

A Small-Town Wedding

Recently I was in a small town in Texas to officiate at the wedding of my niece. While my brother-in-law, Eldon, was in the local hair salon, waiting for his wife to have her hair done, another woman asked him if he was new in town.

He said he was just there for a wedding. The woman said the whole town knew about the wedding, and wondered if the local pastor was doing it.

Eldon replied, "No, my brother-in-law, an Episcopal priest is here and he'll be doing it."

The woman replied, "Well, at least you'll like the minister."

REV. DR. GEORGE H. MARTIN
ROSEMOUNT, MINNESOTA

One of the greatest mysteries of life is how the boy who wasn't good enough to marry the daughter can be the father of the smartest grandchild in the world.

WOODMEN OF THE WORLD

"He's more compatible with his computer than with me."

from JoyfulNoiseletter.com
© Harley L. Schwadron

They Go Together Like a Horse and Carriage:
Marriage Advice, Counseling Stuff, and Help Wanted

According to an old song, it's love and marriage that go together like a "horse and carriage." The song writer responsible for that smarmy couplet probably liked the "marriage" and "carriage" rhyme, which certainly works better than, "Go together like a horse and e-Harmony," or even worse, "Go together like Democrats and Republicans."

Rumor has it that the original lyrics combined "love" with "turtledove," but a marriage counselor let him know that that illusion was too flighty, not permanent enough. So he changed the rhyme scheme to unite "marriage" with the likes of "heritage" and "lineage." Eventually, what really stuck was "mucilage," until it was pointed out that true love, while certainly a bond, probably shouldn't be likened to a gummy adhesive.

Marriage and carriage it is.

THE CYNIC AS MARRIAGE COUNSELOR

"An archeologist is the best husband a woman can have; the older she gets the more interested he is in her."

AGATHA CHRISTIE

"Bachelors know more about women than married men; if they didn't, they'd be married, too."

H. L. MENCKEN

"The most effective way to remember your wife's birthday is to forget it once."

ANONYMOUS

"When a man opens the door of his car for his wife, you can be sure of one thing: either the car is new or the wife is new."

ANONYMOUS

MARRIAGE SUGGESTIONS

"If you want your spouse to listen and pay strict attention to every word you say, talk in your sleep."

VIA REV. KARL R. KRAFT

"Happy marriages begin when we marry the ones we love, and they blossom when we love the ones we marry."

TOM MULLEN

Advice to young people: Don't go for looks; they can deceive. Don't go for wealth; even that fades away. Go for someone who makes you smile because it only takes a smile to make a dark day seem bright. Find the one that makes your heart smile.

from JoyfulNoiseletter.com
© Ed Sullivan

A DAFFY-NITION

A priest readying young candidates for confirmation informs them that the bishop will be coming to test them on how well they know their catechism. The priest instructs them on everything from matrimony to purgatory.

On the appointed day, the bishop conducts an exam. "What's matrimony?" he asks Johnny.

"Matrimony is where the poor souls go to suffer until they're admitted to heaven," Johnny answers.

COLUMNIST TOM RADEMACHER
GRAND RAPIDS (MICHIGAN) *PRESS*

WHEN DINNER BURNS

"The greatest remedy for anger is delay."

REV. ROBERT E. HARRIS
ASHEVILLE, NORTH CAROLINA

"The happiness of married life depends upon making small sacrifices with readiness and cheerfulness."

JOHN SELDEN
APPLE SEEDS

"Anyone who takes himself too seriously always runs the risk of looking ridiculous; anyone who can consistently laugh at himself does not."

VACLAV HAVEL
FIRST PRESIDENT OF THE CZECH REPUBLIC
VIA EDWARD A. BLACK JR.
BROOMFIELD, COLORADO

QUAKERS?

"The formula for a happy marriage is the same as for living in California; when you find a fault, don't dwell on it."

AUTHOR UNKNOWN

A Virtual Reality Wedding

There was a photograph—a bride and groom standing about ten feet apart, facing each other, and each wearing electronic goggles with wires attached to a computer. They were surrounded by a waist-high fence to protect them from falls.

Why? They were getting married in virtual reality. The friends and family gathered to watch, but the couple was saying their vows surrounded by images of who-knows-what, off in another world, through the power and sights and sound that made the viewer breathless and absorbed in the beauty and wonder of the moment.

This is virtual reality.

I have news for the couple. They don't need electronic goggles to get married in virtual reality. On the wedding day, the couple is existing in virtual reality already. Actual reality comes later.

On the wedding day, the bride is adorned in a lavish costume that would have made eight payments on the new car for which she overspent just before she met this guy, because she was depressed that she did not have anyone and would probably die lonely, since she was already twenty-three.

The gown, which takes two hours for a team of six to assemble on her body, creates a vision of loveliness and purity and a fairy tale in which the princess is carried down the aisle on a carpet of bluebirds.

Her hair, which was prepared by a team of experts in a local salon, then transported to the church and reassembled with hair spray upon arrival, looks lavishly like a salad, with flowers and small plants sprouting throughout. She carries in her hands a sort of side salad, matching the vegetation on her head.

Who needs electronics to create something surrealistic? This is virtual reality at its virtually realest.

Of course, the bridegroom is living other than in reality, too. When he sees her coming down the aisle, he doesn't see her in the gown but out of it, sitting in that great new car she had just bought when he met her, and which first attracted him to her.

The virtual reality of the wedding is soon replaced, of course, by the reality of, well, reality.

The gown is dry cleaned and hung up at the parents' home taking up about one-third of useable basement space.

The hair products that so beautified the bride for her groom now take up 95 percent of the bathroom closet, cabinet, and counter space.

The car that caught his eye and caught her man now catches dings from the local mall parking lot and past due notices from the auto loan company.

But the couple is happily married—virtually.

REV. PAUL LINTERN

"I LOVE WEDDINGS"

At the eleventh annual Holy Humor Sunday service (the Sunday after Easter) of Corinth Reformed Church of Hickory, North Carolina, Pastor Robert M. Thompson shared some funny memories of his twenty years in ministry. His sermon was titled: "Church People Are Funny."

"I love weddings and premarital

counseling," Rev. Thompson said. "I remember the bride-to-be who said to me, in all seriousness, 'Why do I need premarital counseling? I've been married twice.'

"Then there was the woman who scored a ninety-ninth percentile on 'hostile' on a temperament test given during premarital counseling. When I pointed out that fact to her, she got really mad! At me!

"That couple stopped the counseling, left the church, and got married elsewhere. A couple of years ago, I ran into her now ex-husband. He said, 'I think God was trying to tell me something through you that day.'

"The most memorable wedding moment was in a wedding that looked like trouble from the start of the procession. The bride felt her veil slipping backwards and reached up with her hand to stabilize it.

"For the next twenty minutes, especially during the prayers, she, the maid of honor, and a bridesmaid tried to steady the veil. Finally, during the recessional, she snatched the veil out of her hair and handed it to her mother.

"I'm guessing a very few people that day heard a word I said."

NEW COUPLE'S ADVICE FROM Noah

Everything you really need to know can be learned from Noah's Ark:

- ♥ Plan ahead. It wasn't raining when Noah built the Ark.
- ♥ Stay fit. When you're six hundred years old, someone might ask you to do something really big.
- ♥ Don't listen to critics. Do what has to be done.
- ♥ Build on high ground.
- ♥ For safety's sake, travel in pairs.
- ♥ Two heads are better than one.
- ♥ Take care of your animals as if they were the last ones on earth.
- ♥ Don't forget that we're all in the same boat.
- ♥ When the manure gets really deep, don't sit there and complain. Shovel!
- ♥ Stay below deck during the storm.
- ♥ Remember that the woodpeckers inside are often a bigger threat than the storm outside.
- ♥ Don't miss the boat.
- ♥ No matter how bleak it looks, there's always a rainbow on the other side.

"We videotaped our arguments. Couldn't you just review them and tell us who's right?"

from JoyfulNoiseletter.com
© Harley L. Schwadron

HANDS UP!

Have you heard about the pastor who officiated at so many shotgun weddings that she decided to rename her church "Winchester"?

UNKNOWN

A JOKER IN THE CROWD

When Roger Polt and his wife, Lois, of Marshalltown, Iowa, were college students and engaged to be married many years ago, they attended a "Pre-Cana Conference" with a priest at the Catholic church on campus.

At the conference Polt picked up a Bible and found inside it a sheet of paper listing the following "Biblical Ways to Acquire a Wife," slipped in by an anonymous author:

♥ Have God create a wife for you while you sleep. Note: this will cost you a rib (Genesis 2:21).

♥ Agree to work seven years in exchange for a woman's hand in marriage. Get tricked into marrying the wrong woman. Then work another seven years for the woman you wanted to marry in the first place (Genesis 29:15–30).

♥ Wait for your brother to die. Take his widow (Genesis 38:8).

♥ Find a man with seven daughters and impress him by watering his flock (Exodus 2:16–21).

♥ Purchase a piece of property and get a woman as part of the deal (Ruth 4:4–5).

♥ Go to a party and hide. When the women come out to dance, grab one and carry her off to be your wife (Judges 21:23).

♥ Find an attractive prisoner of war, bring her home, shave her head, trim her nails, and give her new clothes. Then she's yours (Deuteronomy 21:11–13).

♥ Become the emperor of a huge nation and hold a beauty contest (Esther 2:3–4).

♥ When you see someone you like, go home and tell your parents, "I have seen a woman; now get her for me." If your parents question your decision, simply say, "Get her for me. She's the one for me" (Judges 14:1–3).

CASHING IN

A father escorted the bride down the aisle to the waiting groom. The bride then turned and kissed her father and placed something in his hand.

The pastor smiled, and guests in the front pew laughed. The bride had given back her father's credit card.

NANCY TANGNEY
KALAMAZOO, MICHIGAN

BUT SERIOUSLY. . .

"To forgive heals the wound; to forget heals the scar."

P.T. BARNUM

"A good marriage is the union of two forgivers."

RUTH BELL GRAHAM

HAPPILY INCOMPATIBLE

Ruth Bell Graham, the wife of evangelist Billy Graham, was known for her witty remarks.

When asked if she and her famous husband always agreed on everything, she replied, "My goodness, no! If we did, there would be no need for one of us!"

Billy Graham himself once described the secret of their more than sixty-year marriage as follows: "Ruth and I are happily incompatible."

Marriage is nature's way of keeping people from fighting with strangers.

JOSEPH CLARO

BEFORE AND AFTER

"There are times when men don't understand women—before marriage and after marriage."

GEORGE GOLDTRAP

"I knew it was going to be a difficult marriage when we singed each other with the unity candles."

from JoyfulNoiseletter.com
© Jonny Hawkins

WHEN TWO BECOME ONE

From essays by immigrants writing in the
English language for the first time:

- ♥ "I think she is really glad she got
  marinated."
- ♥ "I fell in love with her the first time I
  sawed her."

During a premarital counseling session, a
pastor asked the young groom-to-be, "When
are you thinking about getting married?"
"Constantly," the young man replied.

GEORGE GOLDTRAP
ORMOND-BY-THE-SEA, FLORIDA

PRE-NUPTING

A young couple came into the office of Msgr.
Charles Dollen of Poway, California, to fill
out the prenuptial questions form. The young
man, who had never talked to a priest before,

was nervous, and Msgr. Dollen tried to put him at ease.

When they came to the question, "Are you entering this marriage of your own free will?" there was a long pause. Finally, his fiancée looked at the young man and said, "Put down 'Yes.'"

NORMA SIMS
EUSTIS, FLORIDA

SECOND Thoughts

After a Saturday afternoon wedding service, the bride and the groom approached me and handed me a small white envelope. In it were a thank-you note and a twenty dollar honorarium. The reception was held, and the couple left for their honeymoon.

On the following Thursday, I found an identical envelope, addressed to me, lying on my desk. I was confused. When I opened it, I found another twenty dollars and a note which read, "It was worth more than I thought."

REV. GERALD A. KRUM
ST. JOHN'S EVANGELICAL LUTHERAN CHURCH
LEWISTOWN, PENNSYLVANIA

COUPLE WISDOM

"By all means marry; if you get a good wife, you will become happy; if you get a bad one, you will become a philosopher."

SOCRATES

"Marry someone who makes you laugh. Everything else will fall into place."

DALTON ROBERTS
CHATTANOOGA, TENNESSEE

"Sexiness wears thin after a while, but to be married to a man who makes you laugh every day, ah, now that's a real treat."

JOANNE WOODWARD
VIA M. VILLALOVOS, WHITTIER, CALIFORNIA

"Of course there's something missing in your marriage. You need a theme song."

from JoyfulNoiseletter.com
© Harley L. Schwadron

MARRIAGE BLOOPER

Rev. Philip M. Oriole of the Church of St. John the Baptist, Erie, Pennsylvania, reports that the company that uses a computer to print the church's Sunday bulletin placed a group of "New Parishioners" under "Weddings" as follows:

RONALD & JANICE KUNIK & JENNIFER CIECIERSKI

SPIC AND SPAN

Think you got it bad? In the sixteenth century, most people got married in June because they took their yearly bath in May, and were still smelling pretty good by June— although they were starting to smell, so brides carried a bouquet of flowers to hide the odor.

UNKNOWN
VIA BUD FRIMOTH
PORTLAND, OREGON

FRENCH FRIED?

A woman about to be married in Vermont explained to a friend that she wanted to have wheat, instead of rice, thrown after the wedding because she wanted to add a touch of her home state—Kansas.

"It's a good thing she's not from Idaho," the friend told the woman's fiancé.

LOIS WARD
LONGMONT, COLORADO

SOME TESTIMONIALS

"As for myself, I married Miss Right. I just didn't know her first name was 'Always.'"

RED SKELTON

A bishop who was a missionary in Africa discovered a tribe who had never recorded a baptism, confirmation, or marriage. The bishop proceeded to baptize and confirm everyone in the tribe and married every couple that walked by.

Later, the tribal chief told the missionary that the tribe had never had so much fun. The missionary asked the chief which ceremony they enjoyed the most.

The chief, breaking into a big smile, replied, "The marriage service. We all got new wives!"

PAUL R. COLEMAN
GIBSONIA, PENNSYLVANIA

6

"Isn't that cute? – They're texting their vows."

from JoyfulNoiseletter.com
© Harley L. Schwadron

HERE COMES THE BRIDE, DUM, DUM, DA-DUM:
Of Gowns, Tuxes, Ceremonies, Wedding Cakes, and "I Do's"

That magic moment: The organist hits those familiar notes, the bride's mother rises, the whole congregation follows suit. All eyes turn to the back door, where stands a teary-eyed dad with his gorgeously white-clad "little girl" on his arm. Up front, a gawky young man in his wedding-day duds gets his first glimpse of the woman he's about to love, honor, and— "cherish."

Today's wedding ceremonies often take place outdoors—in backyards and sometimes on Ferris wheels. Sometimes, designer gowns and rented tuxedos have gone the way of "O Promise Me," and "Does anyone know any reason why this couple. . ."

Humor and irony have crept over the God-inspired observance of marriage. Long-time married comedians like Bob Hope reflect on marriage with such one-liners as, "We're happily married. We wake up in the middle of the night and laugh at each other." But face it: there are things about any institution that are fun to laugh at. . .

FOR BETTER, OR WOOF

Lois Blanchard Eades of Dickerson, Tennessee, contributed this poem as a commentary on an article in the *Nashville Banner* about a man who was using his dog as a wedding attendant:

> *My friend endorsed Will Rogers' words profound:*
> *"The more I see of humankind,*
> *the better I like the canine kind,"*
> *so, altar-bound, he ordered a tuxedo for his Setter.*
> *"On second thought," he said, "omit the pants*
> *for fear that might turn a trifle soggy.*
> *My friend was wise to circumvent this chance,*
> *for such a deed would be no more than doggy.*
> *Dog had his day. He middle-aisled it well,*
> *for he'd been taught to heel. He took his place,*
> *for he'd been taught to sit. Who could foretell*
> *that he would lend such dignity and grace*
> *to an occasion which was stranger than your average wedding?*
> *Dog was friend's best man.*

VAS NEW?

My husband and I met when we worked together at Syracuse University, but we got married in the bride's chapel at Riverside Church in New York City.

As we came out of the church after the wedding, we were surprised to see Ernst, a former colleague at Syracuse University, coming up Riverside Drive, since we hadn't any reason to tell him of our wedding plans.

Ernst, who had a German accent, had been known at the university for starting every encounter with "Vas new?" So we weren't surprised when the first thing he said outside the church was, "Vas new?" That was forty-seven years ago.

KITTY KATZELL
MEDFORD, NEW JERSEY

NANCY ON HIS MIND

My father, Buddy Bianco, is a deacon at a Catholic church in Harrington, Delaware. He has officiated at a few marriage ceremonies. In the Rites of Marriage book, the names of the bride and groom are to be spoken at the proper time. They are marked in the book as 'N' and 'N' (for name).

He would type the names on a piece of paper so that he wouldn't forget the names of the bride and groom.

Unfortunately, at one wedding, he called the groom "Nancy," the name of my sister. At another wedding, the wedding of his own son, he called the bride "Nancy" when her name was Mary. I guess, subliminally, he wanted his other daughter, Nancy, to get married.

JEANNE BIANCO
HARRINGTON, DELAWARE

"For better or worse than what?"

A SIGN OF THE TIMES

Outside the church the cameras snapped at the groom and his bride so new.
Behind them was a text displayed: THEY KNOW NOT WHAT THEY DO!

PASTOR DONALD PROUT
WEST PRESTON, VICTORIA, AUSTRALIA

"'Tis more blessed to give than to receive; for example, wedding presents."

H. L. MENCKEN
COMEDY COMES CLEAN

Him vs. Hymn

At a wedding attended by Marvin Breshears of Yakima, Washington, the processional hymn for the seating of the mothers was printed in the wedding bulletin as "Come Undo Me" (instead of "Come Unto Me").

BOB WHITE

WEDDING REhEARSALS

Fr. Frank Weber, pastor of Saint Brendan Parish in Clifton, New Jersey, offered this commentary on wedding rehearsals:

"The majority of wedding rehearsals pull together, but I realize that for many people being in church is like being beamed up to the land of Oz.

"At one rehearsal, after I finished giving some basic lead-in prayers to help the couple know when to move, one nervous father was genuflecting at anything that didn't move, while blessing himself and saying, 'Amen.'

"Toward the end of the rehearsal, the father expressed some shock when he realized that the whole ceremony was done in English. 'Since when did they do away with Latin?' he inquired.

"I replied, 'Since Vatican Council II some thirty years ago.'

"If looks could kill, the ones he got from his wife and daughter, the bride, would have cremated him on the spot."

"ME NEXT!"

A pastor was planning to hold a wedding before the congregation right after the Sunday morning service. But he couldn't remember the names of the couple who were to be married.

"Will those wanting to get married please come down front?" he asked.

Immediately, seven single women, two widows, four widowers, and five single men stepped up.

REV. KARL R. KRAFT
MANTUA, NEW JERSEY

NEW HUSBAND'S LIGHT BULB

How many new husbands does it take to screw in a light bulb?

Only one, but it takes him two weekends and three trips to the hardware store.

"She'll take my name? How do I know
this isn't just an identity theft scheme?"

A Thunderous Kiss

My wife Linda and I both wanted an unforgettable wedding, and we got more than we bargained for! Just ten minutes before we were to walk down the aisle, an electrical storm blew in. Later, as we got to the back of the church to greet our friends, they told us that at the precise moment I kissed my wife, there was a loud thunderclap.

Several folks remarked that it was God's sense of humor. I had finally gotten married for the first time at forty-one! A friend later sent us a plaque which read, Marriages Are Made in Heaven but So Are Thunder and Lightning. How true for us!

Bill Hodge
Black Mountain, North Carolina

LIVING VOWS

The bride and groom wrote some of the lines for their wedding ceremony. But at the wedding, the groom badly botched his lines. I coached him, very quietly, to get out the necessary words.

After the ceremony, the bride asked me if they were really married since he had so badly botched his lines.

"Yes," I told her, "as long as you never get sick."

THE PRIEST

I BEG YOUR PARDON?

A little girl in a Baptist church asked her mother, "Why do they rope off the aisle at a wedding? So the bridegroom can't get away?"

TAL BONHAM

After a wedding, a teacher in a Catholic school asked her teenagers the definition of marriage. A girl answered, "It's a sacrament which ignites a man and a woman."

A REAL RINGER

While officiating at a wedding ceremony at Skyline Christian Church in Idaho Falls, Idaho, minister Thomas Baird asked the groom, "Would you have these vows sealed with the gift of a ring?"

To Baird's astonishment, the groom reached into his pocket, took out a quarter, and flipped it into the air. Catching the quarter, he looked at it and then replied, "Yep."

The wedding ceremony then proceeded to its conclusion.

"Yes or no, John. There's no plea bargaining here!"

from JoyfulNoiseletter.com
© Goddard Sherman

REALLY AND TRULY

The groom, Doug, was very serious and quite nervous when the time came to make his wedding vows to the bride, Donna. After the pastor asked the groom to repeat the phrase, "In the name of God, I Doug, take you, Donna, to be my wife," the groom—staring intently into the bride's eyes—replied, "In the name of Doug, I God, take you, Donna, to be my wife."

When the bride and then the entire congregation burst into laughter, the groom asked, "What did I say?"

Grace Presbyterian Church in Wichita, Kansas, recently announced a new slogan— "Building Bridges." The following blooper subsequently appeared in the church's newsletter: "Building Brides. . .with God All Things Are Possible!"

REV. WARREN J. KEATING
DERBY, KANSAS

AN IRISH WEDDING BLESSING

May the road rise to meet you.
May the wind be always at your back.
May the sun shine warm upon your face,
the rains fall soft upon your fields.
May the light of friendship guide your paths
together.
May the laughter of children grace the halls of
your home.
May the joy of living for one another trip a smile
from your lips,
a twinkle from your eye.
And when eternity beckons, at the end of a life
heaped high with love,
may the good Lord embrace you with arms that
have nurtured you the whole length of your joy-
filled days.
May the gracious God hold you both in the palm
of His hands.
And, today, may the Spirit of Love find a
dwelling place in your hearts.

That Takes the. . .

A cake decorator in New Zealand was asked to inscribe 1 John 4:18—"There is no fear in love, but perfect love casteth out fear"—on a wedding cake. The decorator misread the verse, and when the cake arrived at the wedding reception, it was discovered that John 4:18 was inscribed on the cake. "For thou hast had five husbands, and he whom thou now hast is not thy husband."

HAROLD W. BRETZ
INDIANAPOLIS, INDIANA

A Toast

At a wedding reception attended by four pairs of the divorced and remarried parents and stepparents of the bride and groom, one father rose and toasted the newlyweds as follows: "I wish you the joy and humor of Jesus, good health, longevity, and only one Christmas every year."

"And do you, Bob, agree to the wording of
Alice's pre-nuptial agreement, and do you,
Alice, agree to the wording of Bob's?"

WHOOPS!

After an unusually busy day that included three weddings followed by a funeral, an exhausted pastor in Indianapolis—at the end of the funeral service—congratulated the widow.

After he was assigned to a mission church in a small town in Peru, Fr. Joseph M. Everson presided at his first wedding. The priest, who had just completed several months of Spanish studies, concluded the ceremony with these words: "Go now in peace. This marriage is finished."

LEO L. LINK
MUSKEGON, MICHIGAN

A pastor received the following thank-you note from a newlywed in his congregation: "Dear Pastor: I want to thank you for performing our marriage ceremony. It was beautiful the way you brought my happiness to a conclusion."

REV. DENNIS R. FAKES

SOMETHING FISHY HERE

The preacher at the wedding was an ardent fisherman and forgetful. He asked the groom, "Do you promise to love, honor and cherish this woman?"

"I do," said the groom meekly.

"Okay," said the minister, turning to the bride. "Reel him in!"

JIM REED
THE FUNNY SIDE OF FISHING

Last year more people applied for fishing licenses than marriage licenses. Does that tell you something?

JIM REED
THE FUNNY SIDE OF FISHING

WEDDING SERVICE FOLDER BLOOPER

For those of you who have children and don't know it, we have a nursery downstairs.

SUBMITTED BY DR. GEOFF PANKHURST
TOOWOOMBA, AUSTRALIA

LET THERE BE LIGHT!

Fr. Tom Martin of Mendon, Michigan, was officiating at an evening wedding at a Catholic church in Columbus, Ohio. The groom was Protestant and the bride Catholic. During the ceremony, a thunderstorm arrived and became fiercer while the bride and groom were saying their wedding vows.

Lightning struck the church's power lines, and the lights went out. Then suddenly the lights went on again, just as the bride was saying "I do."

The priest, suspecting that not all of the groom's Protestant family felt comfortable in a Catholic church—particularly one assaulted by thunder and lightning—tried to put everybody at ease. He commented, "Now you know that we Catholics take our wedding vows very seriously."

JOYCE BEDE
KALAMAZOO, MICHIGAN

"The correct response is 'I do' – not 'It's worth a try.'"

IMPERIAL MARGARINE KING

Some years ago, my sister, Eleanor, got married in an Eastern church. It is customary in the Eastern church to place heavy gold crowns on the heads of the bride and groom during the wedding liturgy.

Afterward, her husband, a member of the Dutch Reformed church, remarked, "I felt just like the Imperial Margarine King."

FR. ARCHDEACON WILLIAM B. KUERTICH
UKRAINIAN ORTHODOX CATHOLIC CHURCH
BOONTON, NEW JERSEY

HOT TIME FOR ALL

On a hot summer day, an hour before a scheduled wedding at Nativity of the Lord Jesus Catholic Church in Akron, Ohio, it was discovered that the groom had left the rings at his home in Mogadore, a nearby suburb.

The best man left his coat at church, jumped into his car, and drove to Mogadore to get the rings. When he arrived at the groom's house, he realized that he did not have the house keys, so he broke into the house through a window.

An alert neighbor saw him and called the police, who quickly arrived and arrested him. He told them what he was doing, and they put him into the police car and drove him to the church to verify his story. Happily, the wedding was celebrated with the rings and the best man present.

FR. DAVID HALAIKO
AKRON, OHIO

COUPLE VOWS

J. J. Jasper, announcer for American Family Radio Network, mentioned on the air that he and his girlfriend, Melanie, were going to "say our vows" and get married. A six-year-old girl listening with her mother exclaimed, "Hey, Mommy, they're gonna say their vows. I know mine, too—*A, E, I, O,* and *U*!"

"My lawyer advises me not to answer that."

GERIATRIC CONFESSION

A pastor who had officiated at the marriage
of a couple in their eighties visited them after
they returned from their honeymoon.

"Well, folks, how did you spend your
honeymoon?" the pastor asked.

"Getting out of the car," the wife replied.

ROBERT H. PRATER
ERLANGEN, GERMANY

WED FOR FREE

A dignified-looking man was about to tee
off on the first hole of a golf course when a
stranger approached and asked if he could
join him. After playing several holes, the
stranger said, "We're about evenly matched.
How about playing for two dollars a hole?"

The first man agreed. The stranger won
the remainder of the holes, and after collecting
the bet, he confessed that he was the pro at
a nearby golf course. The first golfer then
confessed that he was a pastor at a local church.

The embarrassed pro apologized profusely and offered to return the money to the pastor. "Oh no," the pastor declined. "There is a moral to this for me. I was a fool to bet with you. Keep your winnings."

"Well, is there anything I can do for you?" the pro asked.

"Sure," the pastor said. "Come to church on Sunday and put your winnings in the offering. And, if you bring your father and mother to church with you, I'll marry them for free."

PATTY WOOTEN

TWO BEST MEN

Joyful Noiseletter consulting editor Rev. Dr. Karl R. Kraft, pastor of Mantua, New Jersey, United Methodist Church, writes, "After almost four decades in the ministry, I've learned never to say, 'I've seen it all.'

"I officiated recently at a wedding where the groom had given the honor of best man to *two* men, who were listed as 'co-best men' in the bulletin.

"At the rehearsal, I asked the two best men if they had decided which one would hand me the ring. They said they hadn't decided yet, but assured me that they would work it out by the wedding the next afternoon.

"At the wedding, when I asked for the rings, I turned to the two best men. They looked at each other, nodded, and proceeded to play one round of 'rock, paper, scissors.'

"The best man closer to the groom won out, so the other best man took the ring out of his pocket and handed it to the closer best man, who handed it to me."

NOT THE BEST OF TIMES

"You can tell that times are bad," the pastor was precise, "when couples are getting married because they need the rice."

PASTOR DONALD PROUT

Firefighter's Wedding

Rev. Paul Lintern, a humorist and frequent contributor to *The Joyful Noiseletter*, is a Lutheran pastor in Mansfield, Ohio. He tells the following story:

Over the course of a hundred-plus weddings, I have had the opportunity to perform ceremonies in many places outside of the traditional church setting.

From exotic Captiva Island overlooking the Gulf Coast in Florida, to a gazebo on the shore of Lake Erie, to a sandbox in a friend's backyard, I have been privileged to officiate (black-and-white striped shirt with a whistle around my neck) at a wide variety of public nuptial ceremonies.

I have officiated at such "theme weddings" as western, poolside, and hippie. I even performed a wedding once at a bridal show in Wooster, Ohio, with a bridal party modeling the latest in fashion, while I modeled the latest in black clergy shirt and black suit.

But my most unusual wedding was at a fire museum last year in Mansfield, Ohio.

The firefighter's museum seemed a logical setting, since the groom was a local firefighter and the couple was on fire for each other. We gathered in a room surrounded by fire trucks and hoses, equipment and uniforms—memorabilia from a century and more of firefighting.

The groom and the groomsmen were dressed in full regalia—carefully scrubbed yellow fireproof coat and pants, with huge boots and air packs and masks, complete with helmet. The bridesmaids also wore the same yellow coats and pants, but with open-toe boots and lace bodice with a series of red bows in place of the air packs.

The bride, arriving in hook and ladder (symbolizing the way her heart was hooked by the bridegroom and that they had almost eloped), had a traditional white wedding dress, but with boots underneath the full hoop skirt and a helmet and air mask replacing the veil.

With Van Halen singing "Jump," (on CD, not live) she jumped off the extended ladder into the antique circular (symbolizing eternal love) safety net, held by the entire wedding party. After the EMTs were called and placed the bride on a backboard, the ceremony continued.

Music included a beautifully presented harp and flute rendition of "Light My Fire," followed by a powerful oboe and guitar version of "St. Elmo's Fire." The father of the bride sang a tearful "Smoke Gets in Your Eyes."

I read scripture passages about being rescued from sin and avoiding the lake of fire, then admonished the whole party to join as one department, working together to fan the flames of the Holy Spirit. The wedding party had recently joined a church that met in the firehouse and called themselves "Ladder-Day Saints."

The vows were very meaningful. They promised to love and cherish each other forever, keeping the embers glowing. They both also promised to quit smoking.

Following the ceremony, a reception was held in the museum, with guests sitting in and on the trucks. I enjoyed a meal atop a vintage 1930 pumper truck, eating smoked sausage and German potato salad.

After the reception, which the last department did not leave until early morning—just to make sure there were no flare-ups—the couple left for a honeymoon in the Smoky Mountains.

7

"Oh, come on, sweetheart, they're just going to evaluate the first hundred days of our marriage."

from JoyfulNoiseletter.com
© Ed Sullivan

HOME ON THE RANGE:
Getting Started, Two > One, Burnt Offerings, and "Oh My Goodness!"

"Where never is heard, a discouraging word. . ."

Now, how realistic is that? Setting up housekeeping is not a piece of cake. Neither is that first meal—unless, the dessert is the defrosted top of your wedding cake.

Speaking of meals, much has been made of new housewives' cooking abilities. TV joke-writer and humorist Martha Bolton has been heard to say, "I can't cook—I use a smoke alarm as a timer," and "My husband Russ says I treat him like he's a god—every meal is a burnt offering."

Not all newly married chaos takes place in the kitchen. There was a recent blurb on the daily news about a young couple's disagreement over which toothbrush was whose. That little skirmish led to one black eye, three visits to a marriage counselor, and a long-distance call to mama.

Can't begin to sympathize with so-called burnt offerings. Cooking proficiency is not included in the couples' application for a marriage license. Just imagine what such a document might look like—with questions like (1) What experience have you had in boiling water? (2) Are you able to punch-in the correct numbers on a standard microwave? (3) Are you comfortable with disguising take-out to imitate home cooked? (4) Do you understand the difference between fast food and slow cooked? Thusly, the list goes on. . . .

And speaking of "roaming buffaloes," we won't even touch the issue of housekeeping.

SIGN ON A PLUMBER'S TRUCK

WE REPAIR WHAT YOUR HUSBAND FIXED.

FOR NEW COUPLES FACING A NEW YEAR

As we face the New Year, let us focus. . .
not on our fears, but on the Father;
not on our failures, but on the Forgiver;
not on our anxieties, but on the Answer;
not on our worries, but on the Way;
not on our troubles, but on the Truth;
not on our liabilities, but on the Light;
not on our scarcities, but on the Supply;
not on our insufficiencies, but on the
Inexhaustible;
not on our obstacles, but on the Omnipotent;
not on our loneliness, but on the Love.

WILLIAM ARTHUR WARD
VIA *APPLE SEEDS*

FREE Tax Advice

IRS auditor to taxpayer: "No, I'm sorry but you can't claim depreciation on your spouse."

REV. KARL R. KRAFT

7-UPS FOR THE JUST-MARRIEDS

Wake-Up
Begin the day with the Lord. It is His day. Rejoice in it.

Dress-Up
Put on a smile. It improves your looks. It says something about your attitude.

Shut-Up
Watch your tongue. Don't gossip. Say nice things. Learn to listen.

Stand-Up
Take a stand for what you believe. Resist evil. Do good.

Look-Up
Open your eyes to the Lord. After all, He is your only Savior.

Reach-Up
Spend time in prayer with your adorations, confessions, thanksgivings and supplications to the Lord.

Lift-Up
Be available to help those in need—serving, supporting and sharing.

REV. WALTER SCHOEDEL AND
WHEAT RIDGE MINISTRIES
RALEIGH, NORTH CAROLINA

HOW COME?

Classified ad in *The Daily Nonpareil,* Council Bluffs, Iowa: LOVELY BRIDLE Gown and Veil, size 10-11, $200. Call 322-6062."

LILLI VORSE
COUNCIL BLUFFS, IOWA

STRANGER. THAN FiCTiON

Excerpt from a religious tract handed on a street corner to Bishop Frank H. Benning, near St. James Anglican Church in Atlanta, Georgia:

"At the age of ten years old, I had accepted Jesus as my savior, and had promised God at that time that I would go to Bible College and serve Him, but as a teenager I decided to flirt with the devil and ended up getting married and living in sin instead."

A MARRiAGE TRuiSM

Married life is full of excitement and frustrations: In the first year of marriage, the man speaks and the woman listens. In the second year, the woman speaks and the man listens. In the third year, they both speak and the neighbors listen.

ANONYMOUS

THEN THERE WERE THREE

One night a wife found her husband standing over their newborn baby's crib. Silently she watched him. As he stood looking down at the sleeping infant, she saw on his face a mixture of emotions: disbelief, doubt, delight, amazement, enchantment, skepticism.

Touched by this unusual display and the deep emotions it aroused, with eyes glistening she slipped her arms around her husband.

"A penny for your thoughts," she whispered in his ear.

"It's absolutely amazing," he replied. "I just can't see how anybody can make a crib like this for only $46.50!"

A DOG'S ADVICE FOR NEWLYWEDS

♥ Never pass up the opportunity to go for a joyride.
♥ Allow the experience of fresh air and the wind in your face to be pure ecstasy.
♥ When loved ones come home, always run to greet them.
♥ Run, romp, and play daily.

- ♥ Take naps and stretch before rising.
- ♥ Eat with gusto and enthusiasm.
- ♥ When you're happy, dance around and wag your entire body.
- ♥ On hot days, drink lots of water and lay under a shady tree.
- ♥ When someone is having a bad day, be silent, sit close by, and nuzzle them gently.
- ♥ Delight in the simple joy of a long walk.
- ♥ If someone scolds you, forgive quickly.
- ♥ If something you want lies buried, dig until you find it.
- ♥ Never pretend to be something you're not.
- ♥ Be loyal.

UNKNOWN

FOR a BRIDE'S Thanksgiving DINNER

May your turkey be plump.
May your potatoes 'n gravy
have nary a lump,
May your yams be delicious,
May your pies take the prize.
May your Thanksgiving dinner
stay off your thighs!

UNKNOWN

KITCHEN MADNESS

She: Why are you mad at me?

He: I'm not mad, I'm dissatisfied.

She: Haven't I been a good wife?

He: You have! You're perfect—except. . .

She: Except what?

He: You don't make french toast like my mother used to make it.

She: What?

He: You don't sprinkle powdered sugar on top like Mom did.

She: Do it yourself.

He: But Mom did it for me.

She: Our vows didn't include powdered sugar.

Him: No, but it did include "For better or for worse."

She: Sugar, I've had enough of worse; let's try better for a while!

The honeymoon is over when the husband calls home to say he'll be late for dinner and the answering machine says it's in the microwave.

8

"The solution is simple. Never, never –
I mean NEVER wallpaper a room together."

The Fight Is On:
Observations, Ups and Downs,
The Good, Bad, and Hmmm. . .

Sure, there are theological differences
between denominations (whoops, "faith
groups"), but one of the quickest ways to
separate the Episcopalians from the Baptists
is to check out their hymnals. If the hymns

have no titles, they are Anglican.

But those who grew up with Baptist-like worship services can remember scanning the songbooks and snickering over some of the titles. There used to be a missionary song entitled "We'll Girdle the Globe," and "Just One Touch" raised adolescent eyebrows, as did "O Why Not Tonight." For others, the prize went to "The Fight Is On."

It was Saint Paul who pushed the fight concept as an apt metaphor for living the Christian life (see 1 Corinthians 9:26, 1 Timothy 6:12, and 2 Timothy 4:7). Those of the Jewish persuasion are well aware of all the fighting that went on between God's people and the rest of the known world.

Speaking of fighting, it was a very honest husband and wife who admitted, "We would have broken up except for the children. Who were the children? Well, she and I were."

Hopefully the guy who passed this joke around wasn't taken seriously:

A couple had been debating the purchase of a new auto for weeks. He wanted a new truck. She wanted a fast little sports car so she could zip through traffic. But everything she liked was way out of their price range.

"Look!" she said. "I want something that

goes from 0 to 200 in four seconds or less. And my birthday is coming up. You could surprise me."

So for her birthday he bought her a brand-new bathroom scale.

Services will be at Downing Funeral Home on Monday the 12th. Please send memorial donations to the Think Before You Say Dumb Things to Your Wife Foundation.

Does DiVoRĊe MaĸE PeOPLE HaPPy?

A survey with the above title, taken by the Institute for American Values in New York City reported that even the most unhappy marriages are salvageable and, with effort and persistence, can be turned into happy marriages. "Among those who rated their marriages as very unhappy, almost eight out of ten who avoided divorce were happily married five years later," the survey reported.

LINCOLN'S WIFE

During the Civil War, Abraham Lincoln said that if it weren't for his little jokes and humorous stories, he couldn't have survived the presidency.

Lincoln was also perturbed because his wife Mary Todd Lincoln frequently went on wild shopping sprees, especially on clothes. Stoically, but with his usual wit, Lincoln once commented, "But Mary, you are spending more than the president of the United States earns."

ON THE DARK SIDE

In a retirement community in Phoenix, Arizona area, a retired man was sitting in the kitchen eating a big breakfast his wife had prepared and reading the morning paper.

His wife, on the other hand, was bustling around the apartment. She had both the dishwasher and the clothes dryer going, and she was pushing the vacuum cleaner.

Her husband looked up from the newspaper and said to her, "I'm proud of you."

"What did you say?" the woman shouted over the noise.

"I'm *proud* of you!" the husband repeated.

"I'm tired of you, too!" she replied.

VIA REV. HENRY E. RILEY, JR.
CHESTERFIELD, VIRGINIA

EVEN DARKER

"I maintain that it should cost as much to get married as it does to get divorced. Make it look like marriage is worth as much as divorce, even if it ain't. That would make the preachers financially independent, like it has the lawyers."

WILL ROGERS
CIRCA 1926

"Every person needs a mate. Things sometimes go wrong that you can't blame on the government."

UNKNOWN

A SOUR MEMORY

A woman applying for a job in a Florida lemon grove was asked by the foreman, "Have you had any experience in picking lemons?"

"Well, yes," she replied. "Two cars and three husbands."

GEORGE GOLDTRAP

THE PAPER ANNIVERSARY

A newly married couple rented a place in a cheap housing complex with paper-thin walls. One evening, when the husband was upstairs and the wife was on the telephone downstairs, the doorbell rang and she went to answer the door.

Her next-door neighbor greeted her, and handed her a roll of toilet paper. "Please give this to your husband," he said. "He's been yelling for it for twenty minutes."

LOIS WARD
LONGMONT, COLORADO

"Your wife will greet you shortly. She's still in the bathroom."

from JoyfulNoiseletter.com
© Tim Oliphant

ANOTHER SIGN OF THE TIMES

"Judging by divorce statistics, today's marriage vows seem to last only until 'debt do us part.'"

CHARLES J. MILAZZO

ANNIVERSARY TIME

Two elderly ranchers in a Texas restaurant were discussing their cattle and horses when the conversation turned to their spouses.

One rancher asked his friend, "Billy Bob, aren't you and Sue celebrating your fiftieth wedding anniversary soon?"

"We sure are," Billy Bob replied.

"Are you going to do anything special to celebrate?" his friend asked.

Billy Bob considered the question and then replied, "For our twenty-fifth anniversary, I took Sue to San Antonio. I was thinking for our fiftieth anniversary, I'd go back down there and get her."

NORMA SIMS

HUSBAND OBSERVATIONS

Al Karlstom of Champaign, Illinois, went
into a Chicago hospital recently for some
tests and overheard some interesting
conversations among staff members.

A newly married nurse told an older floor
supervisor on an elevator: "My husband is an
angel."

"You are really fortunate," the supervisor
replied. "Mine is still living."

One nurse asked another nurse: "Why
don't they put pictures of missing husbands
on beer cans?"

And another nurse describes a young
doctor as follows: "If he's God's gift to
women, God must shop at Walmart."

BONE OF CONTENTION

The congregation of the First Methodist
Church of Houston, Texas, presented its
distinguished pastor, Dr. Charles Allen, with
a new color television set on an anniversary

Sunday. That afternoon, Dr. Allen settled in his easy chair to watch the Raiders play the Cowboys.

Mrs. Allen spoke gently to her husband, suggesting that perhaps the congregation did not present them with a new set for watching football on the Lord's Day.

"Don't think a thing about it, dear," said Dr. Allen. "Just leave it where it is—Billy Graham will be coming on any minute now."

SHERWOOD ELLIOT WIRT
THE BOOK OF JOY

The Talking Frog

An old man was going fishing. He was walking along a country road toward the lake when he suddenly heard a voice calling out.

He looked around everywhere, but could see no one. So he proceeded down the road with his fishing pole.

Again he heard a voice calling out. He looked around but could still see no one. The voice seemed to be coming from the tall grass near a tree.

Investigating further, he saw a frog in the grass near the tree. The frog looked up at him and pleaded, "Please pick me up and kiss me, sir, and I'll turn into a beautiful young bride!"

So the old fisherman picked up the frog gently, put her in his coat pocket, and proceeded toward the lake.

The frog in his coat pocket was hopping mad. "What's the matter with you, man?" the frog shouted. "I told you that if you kissed me, I'd turn into a beautiful young bride!"

"Thanks. I appreciate the offer," the old fisherman replied. "But at my age, I'd rather have a talking frog."

THE FAMILY CIRCUS

"Where were we while all this
was goin' on?"

JESUS LOVES THE LITTLE CHILDREN: The Mouths of Babes, Heads Up Kids, and "He Said What?"

Little girls with their priorities straight used to jump rope to this jingle: "First comes love, then comes marriage, then comes a baby in a baby carriage."

As those little girls got older and had children of their own, the reality of parenthood came closer home, causing one of them to observe in later years, "Children are a great comfort in your old age—and they help you reach it faster, too." The dad of a ten-year-old recently reported, "Ask your child what he wants for dinner only if he's buying."

"They are precious in His sight," could cause the mother of a precocious two-year-old to exclaim, "Yeah, but it's when he's out of sight that scares me."

The other Sunday morning, Pastor Ben Norris held a squirming newborn in his arms and spoke over the child's crying to his parents and grandparents, an uncle and a couple of aunts. "The sounds emanating from little Christopher are God's way of allowing him to register his needs, his feelings, and in no small way, his approval or disapproval of the way you're raising him."

After service, Christopher's father was overheard declaring, "Wow, he's got opinions now—think how it'll be when he's sixteen!"

Why ARROWS?

"What I don't get about angels is why, when someone is in love, they shoot arrows at him or her."

LIZZIE, AGE 6

IT'S ALL B&W

A six-year-old girl who was attending her first wedding asked her mother, "Why is the bride wearing white?"

The mother replied, "Because white is the color of happiness, and a wedding day is a happy day."

"Then why is the man she is marrying wearing black?" the girl asked.

TOM LITTLEJOHN
PONTOTOC, MISSISSIPPI

GOOD QUESTIONS

~~~~~~~~~~~~~~~~~~~~~~~~~~~~~~~~~~

Bruce C. Thompson of Severna Park, Maryland, tells the story of a father who was trying, with difficulty, to explain the concept of marriage to his little daughter. He finally got out the wedding album, hoping to explain the wedding service with pictures.

After they finished looking through the album, the little girl asked, "Oh, is that when Mommy came to work for us?"

My daughter and son-in-law, Sara and Dick Hart, are missionaries in Cochabamba, Bolivia. At Christmastime last year, their seven-year-old son, Daniel, asked his father, "Dad, why would someone want to marry Christmas?"

MIRIAM MURDOCK
CHAPEL HILL, NORTH CAROLINA

KID BRIEFS

A mother's five- and six-year-old daughters were "playing wedding." She overhead these wedding vows: "You have the right to remain silent. Anything you say may be held against you. You have the right to have an attorney present. You may kiss the bride."

A little girl was allowed to attend a wedding for the first time. Her mother explained to the restless little girl that the church was God's house, and she had to be quiet.

On the way to the reception, the girl asked, "Is God going to be at the reception, too?"

NORMA SIMS

A five-year-old boy told his Sunday school teacher, "When I'm done with kindergarten, I'm going to find me a wife—not before."

NORMA SIMS

A Sunday school teacher asked her class if they knew what Jesus said about marriage at the wedding in Cana.

A small boy replied, "Father, forgive them, for they know not what they do."

RALPH ROY
VERO BEACH, FLORIDA

MARVIN'S BED

When it was time for Marvin, age six, to say his bedtime prayers, his mother found him sitting on his bed looking worried. She asked what was troubling him.

"I don't know what'll happen with this bed when I get married," he replied. "How will my wife fit in?"

A Sister Thing

Jenny Mars was trying to put her six children in the car in the parking lot of St. David Parish, Willow Grove, Pennsylvania, when Sister Prudens came over to help.

Jenny's six-year-old daughter, Chrissy, asked the nun: "Sister, what's that on your head?"

"That's a habit," Sister Prudens replied.

"What's a habit?" Chrissy asked.

"It's a veil—you know, like when you get married and you wear a veil," the nun answered.

"Chrissy," her mother explained, "when women become sisters, they get married to Jesus."

"Oh!" the little girl said, then looking at Sr. Prudens, added, "I'm sorry your husband died."

WEDDING DAY

Little Tony was in his uncle's wedding. As he came down the aisle during the ceremony, he carefully took two steps, then stopped and turned to the congregation. When facing the crowd he held his hands up like claws and roared loudly. So it went—*step, step, turn, roar, step, step, turn, roar*—all the way down the aisle.

As you can imagine, the congregation was near tears from laughing. By the time little Tony reached the altar, he was near tears too. When later asked what he was doing, the boy sniffed and said, "I was being the ring bear."

UNKNOWN

"IF I COULD REACH UP AND HOLD A STAR FOR EVERY TIME YOU MADE ME SMILE..."

"...I would be holding the entire
evening sky in the palm of my hand."

from JoyfulNoiseletter.com
© Bil Keane

Smoke Gets in Your Eyes:
The Long Haul, Remember When? and So On

One doctor's prescription to keep romance
in your marriage is—on occasion—to let
the smoke get in your eyes. That's probably
good advice regardless of age, but it will

certainly come in handy when the flame is a bit lower than it once was, and the wind gusts down the chimney of your life. There may be a puff of ashes to annoy, but a whiff of smoke will cloud out some of his and/or your imperfections.

The prophet Isaiah reports that the presence of smoke was once an indication of God's presence (Isaiah 6:4). May all of our homes and relationship allow for a bit of smoke.

A Beatitude

"Blessed are the husband and wife who continue to be affectionate and loving after the wedding bells have ceased ringing."

Reality Programming

A long-married woman proudly told her friend, "I'm responsible for making my husband a millionaire."

"Well, what was he before he married you?" the friend asked.

"A billionaire."

A University of Oregon study has found that humor helps marriages last. John and D. J. Rawlings, who have been married for fifty-two years, interviewed seventy couples who had been married an average of nineteen years. Each couple used humor and laughter to avoid conflict or to release tensions.

ANDY FISHER
DENVILLE, NEW JERSEY

The preacher says: "Let no man put asunder"—and two-thirds of the married world is asunder in less than three months.

PERFECT MATCHES

~~~~~~~~~~~~~~~~~~~~~~~~~~~~~~~~~~~

Overheard in a cafeteria line: "My wife never lies about her age. She just tells everyone she's as old as I am. Then she lies about my age." To which the wife admitted, "I was born in 1962. True. And the room next to me was 1963."

"Everybody goes through tough times. I don't know anybody who doesn't. Faith is how you combat them and handle them. . . I have a great wife. If I could have seen God one week before I got married and had written down on a piece of paper what I wanted for a wife, He could have not have given me a better one than the one I have."

TOMMY LASORDA
FORMER MANAGER, LOS ANGELES DODGERS

No Communication

A woman went to a lawyer and said, "I want to get a divorce!"

The lawyer asked, "Does your husband have any grounds?"

"Yes," she replied. "About twenty acres."

"That's not what I meant," the lawyer said. "Does he have a grudge?"

"No," she said. "Just a carport."

"What I meant was, does he beat you up?" the lawyer said.

"No, I get up first every morning," she replied.

"So just what is your problem?" the frustrated lawyer asked.

"My husband says we can't communicate!"

REV. SAM LASWELL
REDFORD, MICHIGAN

A Prayer for the Married

"Lord, when we are wrong, make us willing to change. When we are right, make us easy to live with."

PETER MARSHALL

How to Keep That "Just Married" Look

The Pasta Diet guarantees weight loss:
   1) You walka pasta the bakery.
   2) You walka pasta da candy store.
   3) You walka pasta da ice cream shop.
   4) You walka pasta da pizza parlor.
   5) You walka pasta da fridge.

RISË SAMRA
HALLANDALE BEACH, FLORIDA

from JoyfulNoiseletter.com
© Ed Sullivan

MIDDLE-AGED HUSBANDS

Palmer Stiles and I were married not long ago. We thought *Joyful Noiseletter* readers would enjoy this story:

"Three middle-aged ladies were waiting in line at a checkout counter in a grocery store. One was talking about her recent marriage and how wonderful her new husband was. She said he waits on her hand and foot and takes her many places.

"The second lady also said her husband took good care of her, and she never had to lift a hand to mop or scrub or clean the house. The third lady also bragged that her husband treats her like a queen.

"A young girl overheard the women's conversations and asked them quite seriously, 'How can I get one of them for my mother?'"

ROSE STILES
MELBOURNE, FLORIDA

HUSBAND CHATTER

A husband read an article to his wife about how many words women use a day—thirty thousand to a man's fifteen thousand. The wife replied, "The reason has to be because we have to repeat everything to men."

The husband turned to his wife and asked, "What?"

Observations on marriage from unknown author, via George Goldtrap of Ormond-by-the-Sea, Florida:

"Marriage: First year—man speaks, woman listens. Second year—woman speaks, man listens. Third year—both speak, the neighbors listen."

Before marriage, men lie awake all night thinking about something you said. After marriage men fall asleep before you finish talking.

There once was a man who muttered a few words in the church and found himself married. A few years later he muttered something in his sleep and found himself divorced.

"The best way to get most husbands to do something is to suggest that perhaps they're too old to do it."

ANNE BANCROFT

AFTER SOME YEARS. . .

A man went to see his pastor about getting a divorce. The pastor, who knew the man's wife, said, "Now why would you want to divorce such a lovely wife? She is soft and gentle and also beautiful. I don't understand what you have to complain about."

The man took off his shoe and showed it to the pastor. "See this shoe?" he asked. "The leather is soft and gentle and the craftsmanship is beautiful. But I'm the only one who knows it pinches."

"We have two choices for Valentine's Day: we can fly away by private jet to a romantic meal in Bali, or we can plunk down 12 bucks for the church's spaghetti supper."

from JoyfulNoiseletter.com
© Ed Sullivan

STILL BLISS

The doctor was giving an eighty-five-year-old retired pharmacist his annual physical examination. The doctor said, "You are really doing quite well—but have you told me everything?"

"Well," said the pharmacist, "I'm really feeling great, and God is looking after me."

"What do you mean by that?" inquired the doctor.

"Every time I get up during the night to go to the bathroom, the Lord turns on the light for me. It doesn't matter if I get up once or ten times during the night, the Lord always turns on the light for me."

When the examination was finished, the doctor told the pharmacist's wife he would like to visit with her about her husband.

"What did you find wrong, doctor?" asked the wife.

"Nothing I can find physically, but mentally, I think your husband is developing some problems. He tells me that every time he gets up to go to the bathroom during the night, the Lord turns on the light for him."

"Oh my goodness!" exclaimed the wife. "He's been getting into our refrigerator again!"

BEATING THE DEVIL

This story from Rev. Dr. Jack Miller of Arnold, Missouri, can be told with either a little old man or a little old woman confronting the devil.

One day the devil decided to visit a small country church. He threw open the church door and strolled in like he owned the place. People were falling over themselves trying to get out of the building.

They ran out the doors and dived through windows to get away from the devil—with the exception of a little old man (little old woman) sitting in the front pew.

The devil came up to him (her) and said, "Do you know who I am?"

"Yes," came the reply.

"Aren't you afraid of me?" the devil demanded.

"No," the old man (woman) replied. "I'm not afraid of you because for the past thirty years I've been married to your sister (brother)."

JINGLE BELLS?

Rick Moore of the Crimson River Quartet, Mission Viejo, California, tells this true story:

A Southern gospel group had arrived home from a singing tour and were called by the widow of a man in their church who had just passed away. The widow asked them to sing three of her husband's favorite songs at the funeral: "In the Garden," "Amazing Grace," and "Jingle Bells."

The group leader had misgivings about singing "Jingle Bells" at a funeral, but when the widow insisted that her husband loved the song, he agreed to sing it, but told her that they would be singing it "real slow."

At the funeral service, the group sang all three songs, including "Jingle Bells," slowly and mournfully. Afterward, the widow thanked the group for singing, and addedn "Oh, I remember the name of the song my husband liked so much. It wasn't "Jingle Bells;" it was "When They Ring Those Golden Bells."

MARITAL HEROICS

A Vatican official, who thinks that married couples who stay together in these modern times are "heroic," has proposed that more married couples be canonized as saints to be role models.

Writing in the Vatican newspaper, *L'Osservatore Romano,* Msgr. Helmut Moll commented, "Staying together in good times and in bad, in sickness and in health, shows a heroic degree of virtue." He observed that some married couples, usually martyrs, are already included in the Catholic Church's long list of saints, usually celibates.

Any nominations for Valentine's Day? Write to: Msgr. Helmut Moll, Congregation for Sainthood Causes, Palazzo, Delle Congregazioni, Piazzo Pio X11-10, 00193 Rome.

A WiFE'S LeGaCy

The wife of an old preacher in Kansas was afraid to fly, but finally summoned the courage to take a flight to Florida to visit her daughter. At the airport, she handed her husband a letter. On the envelope she had written, "Open only in case of a crash."

When he returned home, the old preacher couldn't resist the temptation and opened the letter. "If there is a crash, look under our bed. You'll find a box. Open the box."

He looked under the bed, opened the box, and found three eggs and a large stack of one hundred dollar bills.

He was mystified. When his wife returned intact from Florida, the old preacher confessed that curiosity had gotten the best of him and he had opened both the envelope and the box. "But honey, I don't understand," he said. "Why the three eggs and the one hundred dollar bills?"

"Well, honey," she replied. "When you first started preaching, every time you laid an egg and preached a poor sermon, I'd put an egg in the box."

"All these years I've preached and I got
only three eggs?" he said. "That's not bad.
But I still don't understand the stack of one
hundred dollar bills."

"When you get a dozen, you gotta sell,"
she said.

REV. WARREN KEATING
DERBY, KANSAS

HIS AND HERS EPITAPHS

She lived with her husband
fifty years and died
in the confident hope
of a better life.

Here lies my wife
in earthly mould
who when she lived
did naught but scold.

Good friends, go softly
in your walking
lest she should wake
and rise up talking.

"Forty-three years, Emma, and you still knock my socks off. Happy Valentine's Day."

PRAISE GOD, FROM WHOM ALL BLESSINGS FLOW:
Generally Speaking, Marriage Observations, and Amen

"All creatures here below." That's us! That's you and yours. That's what love, romance, and marriage are all about. It's us creatures down here on planet earth recognizing that all the good stuff of life comes down from above—from Father God, who is worthy of our praise!

It's a concept that has to be recognized by newlyweds, long-timers, second-time-arounders, the divorced, the never-married, and the been-too-long married. Maybe it's best summed up by Marrying Sam, the back-woodsy preacher in the old Lil' Abner comic strip when all the Dogpatch characters came to Abner and Daisy Mae's nuptials. Marrying Sam, in his well-worn coat and stand-up collar, explained to those assembled, "Ya heard this here couple say, 'For richer 'n for poorer,' well I say for them 'poorer' is only financial. Cast yore eyeballs around here and see what the good Lord has given them—and us. Pa-raise the Lord!"

Superb advice.

THINGS THAT SPELL
WEDDING TROUBLE

Humorist Paul Lintern, a Lutheran pastor in Mansfield, Ohio, and consulting editor to *The Joyful Noiseletter*, offers the following warning signs at a wedding:

After officiating (as a referee, as in umpire, as in field judge) at many weddings, I have discovered several signs that indicate that there might be some difficulties in the marriage, signs that may forecast troubled times ahead.

Take the word of this pastor for it. If you notice any of these circumstances at a wedding you attend or plan, beware:

♥ The processional song chosen is from a Metallica album.
♥ The mother of the bride asks whether the wedding will be over in time to get to bingo.
♥ The time of the wedding must remain flexible because the groom's parole hearing is set for that morning.
♥ The unity candle goes out.

- ♥ The couple chooses as its scripture passage the story of Cain and Abel or of King David arranging the death of Uriah the Hittite in order to have the man's wife, Bathsheba.
- ♥ Three fathers arrive to usher the bride down the aisle.
- ♥ The ushers are reluctant to leave their automatic weapons at home.
- ♥ The bride considers the best man better.
- ♥ During the vow, the groom calls the bride by his former girlfriend's name.
- ♥ The couple argues over who will get custody of the unity candle.
- ♥ During a reflective time in the ceremony, the soloist sings about a brick house.
- ♥ Just before the vow, the groom asks, "Is this like, really official? Like, how easy is it to back out?"
- ♥ The videographer's notebook has the address of *America's Funniest Home Videos*.
- ♥ The bride's pager goes off, and she has to run to the office for an "important meeting."
- ♥ Two pews of pregnant women sob uncontrollably as the groom says, "I do."
- ♥ The caterer yells, "Can you hurry up the sermon, preacher? These croissants won't stay fresh all day."

- ♥ The couple fights over the day being ruined because one of them forgot to order the limousine.
- ♥ The recessional hymn is "Turn Back O Man, Foreswear Thy Foolish Ways."
- ♥ The solo sung during the lighting of the unity candle is Frank Sinatra's "My Way."
- ♥ The bridesmaids' dresses have more chains than lace.
- ♥ The vow ends with "as long as we both feel like it."

Four Too Many

A missionary heard about a native who had five wives. "You are violating a law of God," the missionary said. "You must go and tell four of those women they can no longer live here or consider you to be their husband."

The native thought a few moments, then said, "Me wait here. You tell 'em."

TAL BONHAM

"It is more blessed to forgive than to receive."

A HUSBANDLY DUTY

Helping his wife wash the dishes, a not-too-long-wed husband protested, "This isn't a man's job."

"Oh yes it is," his wife retorted, quoting 2 Kings 21:13: "I will wipe Jerusalem as a man wipeth a dish, wiping it, and turning it upside down."

TAL BONHAM

BLUSHING WOULD-BE BRIDE

A maiden lady in her seventies, in commenting on her church's small congregation: "Why, it's so bad in our church on Sundays that when the minister says 'dearly beloved,' I positively blush."

REV. CLIFFORD WHITE
OAKWOOD, ONTARIO

FOR BRIDES AND GROOMS:
TO BE READ TOGETHER

The Lord is the joy of my life, I shall never be
    bored.
He brings me into the fellowship of happy
    friends.
He gives me ecstatic confidence;
He enchants my soul.
He leads me in the way of jubilance for His
    own great praise.
Yea though I struggle through the experience
    of gloom,
I will fear no sadness; the joy of the Lord is
    with me;
Thy grace and Thy cheer, they delight me.
Thou preparest a table before me in the
    presence of the prophets of gloom.
Thou anointest my head with gladness.
My heart bubbles over with joy.
Surely delight and rapture shall follow me all
    the days of my life;
And I shall rejoice in the presence of the
Lord always.

"Do you have a sympathy card for someone whose husband has retired?"

GOD ADS

~~~~~~~~~~~~~~~~~~~~~

LOVED THE WEDDING, INVITE ME TO THE
MARRIAGE. GOD

NEED A MARRIAGE COUNSELOR? I'M
AVAILABLE. GOD

DONNA LAMBERT

FOR WHAT IT'S WORTH

~~~~~~~~~~~~~~~~~~~~~

In many Eastern European countries, celibate
Latin-rite Catholic priests live peaceably
in rectories near the homes of Eastern-rite
Byzantine Catholic priests who are married.
The Eastern-rite married priests teasingly
refer to the rectories of the celibate priests as
"Homes for Unwed Fathers."

A FREE MAN

A married couple was celebrating their fiftieth anniversary in a church social hall. The wife was smiling, but the husband had tears in his eyes. The wife asked the husband why he was crying.

The husband replied, "Fifty years ago today, your daddy put a shotgun to my head, and said that if I didn't marry you, he'd put me in jail for the next fifty years. If I had listened to him, I'd be a free man tomorrow."

GEORGE GOLDTRAP

RIGHT YOU ARE, HARRY

"A man who can't be loyal to his wife and family can't be trusted anywhere."

PRESIDENT HARRY S. TRUMAN

"I can't help it; I just love watching him cook his own dinner."

from JoyfulNoiseletter.com
© Marty Bucella

KEEPING YOU AWAKE?

A man went to a physician about his snoring.

"Does it disturb your wife that much?" the doctor asked.

"My wife?" the man replied. "It disturbs the whole congregation."

VIA ROBERT PRATER

HIS AND HERS HUMOR BY J. J. JASPER

J. J. Jasper's videocassette, *J. J. Jasper World Tour—One Night Only,* begins with this announcement:

"Caution: The Surgeon General suggests that you go without sleep for three hours before watching this video. During this video, you may become light-headed, disoriented, nauseous, or experience sudden loss of hair."

The Christian comic, who is the popular morning disc jockey for American Family Radio Network in Tupelo, Mississippi, then proceeds to offer up a variety of one-liners and down-home anecdotes like this:

♥ "If a man is alone in the woods with no woman to hear him, when he says something, is he still wrong?
♥ "I found an incredible cologne that makes me irresistible to women—it smells like Wal-Mart."

SOONER OR LATER

Donald D. Kaynor of Battle Creek, Michigan, sent along this item:

When an elderly spinster died, her family could not come up with a suitable epitaph for her gravestone. One of the family remembered that a cousin was a sportswriter for a newspaper and asked him to compose the epitaph. He wrote:

HERE LIES THE BONES OF MARY JONES.
HER LIFE IT KNEW NO TERROR.
BORN AN OLD MAID, DIED AN OLD MAID—
NO RUNS, NO HITS, NO ERRORS

JN consulting editor Steve Feldman of Jefferson City, Missouri, has asked his wife to put the following epitaph on his tombstone when he dies:

To Be Continued